The Abundance Economy
THE ABUNDANCE INNOVATION FRAMEWORK

Eight New Business Areas to build
an Abundant Organization
in the 21st Century

Edition 2023

Author

Virginie Glaenzer

With the Contribution of Jean M. Russell

Virginie Glaenzer

Table of Content

FORWARD	**5**
A STORY OF ABUNDANCE	**7**
INTRODUCTION	**12**
CHAPTER ONE: QUESTIONING OUR ECONOMIC LEGACY	**20**
CHAPTER TWO: WEALTH AND HEALTH	**36**
What if wealth is like health but for the social body?	36
Distinguishing between Rival and Non-Rival	37
Social and Technological Opportunities	39
Centralization and Decentralization	40
CHAPTER THREE: REVISITING SCIENCE AND NATURE	**42**
New Science and Other Ways of Knowing	46
New Understanding of Genetics and HGT	47
New Understanding of Microbiology	49
New Understanding of Fungus	51
New Understanding of Forests	52
And Other Interesting Learnings about Humans	53

How Science Has Evolved   56

CHAPTER FOUR: WHAT IS ABUNDANCE?   65

  The Layers of Abundance   66

    Understanding   66

    Perspective   69

    Feeling   70

    Practical Way of Living   70

  Principles of abundance on a finite planet   72

CHAPTER FIVE: THE NEW ECONOMY   77

  The Business of Abundance   77

  What Business Models Can We Learn From Nature?   83

  The New Economy Of Abundance   88

    Abundance Technology   89

    Funding Abundance: Crowd Platforms   91

    Investable Wealth Abundance 94

CHAPTER SIX: THE ABUNDANT FRAMEWORK 99

  The Abundance Innovation Framework   99

  Eight Circles Of Abundance   105

  Abundance Approach   118

  Forms of "Resource" for the Cash Flow Game 120

New Forms of Abundant Business Models   131

CHAPTER SEVEN: EXAMPLES OF ABUNDANT BUSINESSES   **135**

CONCLUSION   **143**

A STORY OF ABUNDANCE - CONTINUED.   **146**

ABOUT THE AUTHOR   **157**

Virginie Glaenzer

FORWARD

The survival struggle we inherited has brought our human spirit to a test, and exhausted our collective ability to create a world where everyone can thrive.

In our quest to see what is possible and unseen, through my personal and professional experiences I spend time deconstructing my conditioned filters, analyzing the way in which I've been taught to perceive in order to discover a new worldview.

I wrote this book because I am driven by the desire to translate the innovations I see in abundance into accessible forms that are useful to people who, like me, are always on the lookout for alternatives.

I believe that the truth seekers, the misfits, the poets, the builders, and the outsiders are the ones who will shape the future.

My aim is to offer a way for anyone to reflect on their lives, and find new ways to live them.

Throughout this book you will find two format-coded sets of contents inviting you to discover your own path.

Bold highlight: challenging ideas to consider.

<u>Gold highlight: Invitation to self-reflection.</u>

Virginie Glaenzer

A STORY OF ABUNDANCE

They could hear birds chirping outside the window. After the harsh winter, spring had finally arrived and buds were blossoming on the fruit trees.

On the nightstand lay a small, hand-made, recycled paper journal with a pressed bird design on the cover. They sat straight up, grabbed the journal, opened it, and read the last written words. Whispering the words, they read: *I'm grateful for the abundance all around. Let go of what you know, and you shall see what is.*

After getting dressed, they sat down at the kitchen table.

"Here you go", said Finley offering them a fresh cup of coffee.

"Thank you! I really need that." they replied with a smile while thinking *"Abundance is all around."*

Morning talk and a kiss were quickly followed by an exit off the front porch. The front garden was a wild and flourishing place. The potager garden grew all sorts of vegetables, herbs, and flowers. Natural ecosystems were flourishing under the permaculture's abundance approach and methodology. The morning light glinted off the golden pollen in the air as bees buzzed—swarm-like—around the flowers.

Taking Myrill Street, they walked several blocks to arrive at Martin's Treasures, one of their favorite shops. Martin, the owner, was standing in front of the store arranging a colored painting made out of fruits and vegetables.

"Good morning, Martin. How are you doing today?" They asked as they slowed their rapid pace.

"Hey! Great! How are you doing, River!" Martin grabbed one of the biggest apples and handed it to them. "Here, have a snack! Lots of good energy!"

"Thank you! That's very generous of you!"

"You know what the farmer says: I can be generous because I have what I need", replied Martin.

River started thinking, "What if…abundance isn't turning everything into gold or living with a giant hoard of treasures, but having what you need when you need it without taking from others?"

After a brisk fifteen-minute walk, River was sitting at their desk. The practice of co-creating with multiple organizations and teams had become commonplace. 20 years ago people used to call it consulting or freelancing but today, in the abundance economy that had emerged, it was just common work. River felt fortunate to have so many options available. They had an abundance of ideas and opportunities to work with.

Today, people's time and attention were valued. For example, after spending one hour online and sharing with their network a few posts of an organization they felt strongly about, they were rewarded for their time and attention with digital coins. These coins could be spent on items at Martin's shop, kept in their digital wallet, or exchanged with other currencies.

In their work, River felt valued and had a strong sense of belonging because they could be themselves. River performed a wide variety of jobs: they designed logos for a couple of organizations, led a team for another one, and worked as a manual laborer for three hours a week. Their wealth was made up of a variety of sources including: tradeable coins and international currencies, sweat-equity accounting, growing food, traded clothing, building artifacts, and unique natural resources.

Later at night, River and Finely entertained a few friends over dinner, and they discussed business plans and models while they ate.

"The stories we tell ourselves run deep," one friend said, "Remember how we used to tell ourselves stories about living in a threatening world, and then how we used to build defenses, even if we never used them?"

"In the last company where I worked full time, back when that was a thing, and before they went under," added another friend, "I clearly remember how we were always told competition was stiff. It made people aggressive and feel stuck. Everyone seemed defensive and hostile. It was so exhausting. Everyone had burnout."

River concluded, "It serves us well to keep asking whether the stories we have been telling ourselves have a relation to the actual threats at hand or if we have created illusions and run with them."

...To be continued in the last chapter of the book.

INTRODUCTION

This book challenges our beliefs by asking this question: Is economics about scarcity or about resource allocation?

For the past 100 years, business schools have taught Economics as *"A social science which is concerned with the production, distribution, and consumption of goods and services and is the study of how individuals, businesses, governments, and nations make choices about how to allocate resources."*[1]

Given the world we see around us, we would benefit from looking deeper.

When we challenge our beliefs and the filters we see through, our understanding can also change. Something else, some other result, might become possible.

---

[1] Investopia

The core hidden assumption of most thinking in economics is that the fundamental questions of resource allocation are all about scarcity.

Thus all of the tooling, including the monetary system itself, operates under that assumption. When we look at all the economic models created under the ideologies of capitalism, socialism, or communism, these models have three things in common: they focus on scarce resources, their national currency is the medium of exchange, and wealth is defined solely as monetary accumulation, with money offering us a nearly universal measure for wealth.[2]

Furthermore, many of the assumptions about human behavior in the context of scarcity (e.g. competitiveness) upon which the economic system is designed, also turn out to be false.

---

[2] Arthur Brock, founder of Holochain

In *Paradise Built in Hell: The Extraordinary Communities that Arise in Disaster*[3], Rebecca Solnit covers numerous disasters across multiple continents and time to reveal that even in places where it seems like resources are quite scarce, humans usually lean toward sharing and caring behaviors.

Mutual Aid[4] shows up in sharp contrast to what those in power, during those times, try to warn us against: the hordes of madmen reduced to rabid animals.

<u>Actual historical data shows that, when in crisis, people tend towards self-organizing stone-soup sharing, not riots and mayhem.</u>

---

[3] https://www.goodreads.com/book/show/6444492-a-paradise-built-in-hell

[4] https://en.wikipedia.org/wiki/Mutual_aid_(organization_theory)

Artificial Scarcity

The scarcity assumption makes some sense, because some resources actually are rare or limited, yet it is an insufficient basis on which to think about all resources. And, because of technological advances, more and more of the most crucial resources are no longer limited. When the economy is tooled around the assumption of scarcity, the core success lesson for businesses is to enclose and control some portion of that scarcity. But **this has led to *artificial* scarcity.** The primary example of this is around our notion of Intellectual Property. Information is never scarce. In fact its value tends to grow the more it is shared. But our economy can't handle this fact. Businesses have a hard time making a profit on information resources unless they can enclose access to that information, and thus we have invented an entire system of making something that is fundamentally abundant into something that is artificially scarce. Today, I suggest that the work ahead of us is to figure out how to fully retool the economy, both in its fundamental assumptions and its embodied systems (like the monetary system) into one that can actually handle the true nature of each type of resource, managing rarity where it exists, and amplifying total systems *value* for resources that actually are abundant.

Abundance through Technology

Possibilities exist today that were never imagined by the original architects of economic theory. Factories and integrated international supply chains have created massive material abundance. We have so much material abundance that we have concerns about the abundance of trash we have generated! The Internet has created even more abundance of the fundamental resource of knowledge. What is even more exciting to me are the hints of new social technologies that will allow us to coordinate in ways that surpass the patterns of the industrial age to maintain or even amplify the lived experience of abundance, without generating wealth disparity as a byproduct or destroying the planet.

This is the gift of technology: to expand what is available by enabling some combination of labor and energy with the right materials to get what we need.

Abundance Economics and Technology continues to be an untapped resource because business executives and startup founders schooled in the old era don't know how to navigate in this new era. It's like attempting to drive a Formula One race car with the mindset and tools of driving a horse and carriage. New tools and mindsets are desperately needed, and we all know what happened to those who held tightly to buggy whips!

This book seeks to address that gap.

The new business methods explore the promise of new social technologies.

In this book, we'll be looking at Eight Business Pillars to help an organization operate using the assumptions of abundance economics. I show case studies of current companies that are defeating old mindsets and scarcity beliefs.

I present a new Abundant Innovation Framework and describe how an abundance-focused organization can thrive in the twenty-first century and beyond.

"Tell me how you will measure me, and then I will tell you how I will behave. If you measure me in an illogical way, don't complain about illogical behavior."

— Eli Goldratt.

CHAPTER ONE: QUESTIONING OUR ECONOMIC LEGACY

On the pathway to our opportunities for abundance, I want to cover some of the concerns about how things appear today.

I have some questions about centralization as an outdated approach to allocation.

I also have some questions about wealth: how it is measured, what is made visible and invisible.

What if organizations like Amazon, or even distributed network patterns like open source communities, actually do have the technology to do the computation for allocation in more ethical ways?

Do we have an open source ecosystem planning framework[5] for resource allocation and production?

---

[5] https://www.valueflo.ws/

Nobody in the 1920s could have imagined the information flows possible in the networked world we live in today.

So, what if the side effects of market allocation are not a given we simply must accept?

What if we are already in the middle of upgrading our social technology and computational ability to deliver on these ethics, not by getting rid of market economies but by adding additional social technologies (such as legal structures, funding mechanisms, and software) to support this more ethical framework?

I believe there is now sufficient evidence that these hypotheticals have been revealed as both possible and preferable.

Growth

One of our assumptions worth questioning is the focus on growth. Growth was a stand-in for societal health when we didn't have better ways to measure it, but that isn't serving us well now.

With all this assumed scarcity, we are somehow supposed to keep growing anyway. Few people will disagree on the fact that we've reached many of the limits of our society's growth mindset. Those limits might be about physical resources, as named in Limits to Growth[6].

Is there enough steel to keep making cars like we did in the 70s? No, so we upgraded the materials to ones that aren't as rare.

It may also be about the marketplace limits as described in Death of Demand[7].

How many cans of soda can one person consume in a day? If everyone who wants to drink soda, can drink as much soda as they want, there is still going to be a limit to how much they buy. Thus the growth of that product is finite.

---

[6] https://en.wikipedia.org/wiki/The_Limits_to_Growth

[7] https://www.goodreads.com/book/show/1851089.The_Death_of_Demand

As we upgrade our understanding of market limits, we improve our expectations of what can happen. And of course there are also personal limits. How do we engage with personal needs around health and well-being rather than pushing people into depression by telling them they need to buy ever more, have ever more, and do ever more to be worthy of love and belonging?

The classic measure of growth, the gross domestic product (GDP), doesn't indicate the state of well-being of a population or even the rate of flow within a country. It was originally created to evaluate war strength. It reveals the ability of an economy to go to war (use violence to express will).

How can we create an experience of sufficiency without focusing on growth?

How can we increase efficiency and effectiveness without compromising on the well-being of people and the need for resources to be replenished (trees to grow, for example)?

How do we negotiate resource allocation to create a lived sense of sufficiency while working within the limits of our environment?

We play a game where maybe what we thought was unlimited turns out to have limits and where the abundance we could experience has been made scarce.

Before we show how the game can be adjusted to fit our actual constraints, we examine the current measures used in the game:

Debt Money

Banks aren't just lending money they have stockpiled from deposits. Banks create money through the very act of issuing debts (mortgages and bonds). In other words, money is loaned into existence by the banking system. Banks are not simple intermediaries who keep track of money coming in from some parties and money going out to others. But they actually increase the money supply in the act of issuing loans.[8] This process is well described elsewhere. What is important to our story is the way the tooling matches the assumptions and systemically drives that was assumed as necessary.

Once we question that, it opens the possibility for different approaches to issuance of a medium for measuring value and lubricating exchange.

---

[8] https://www.youtube.com/watch?v=qIxhsF6JLEA

https://education.howthemarketworks.com/how-is-money-created/

https://hackernoon.com/a-cryptocurrency-as-old-as-civilisation-mutual-credit-part-i-sh1y3xn2

Wealth Velocity

Humans tend to respond to scarcity by hoarding what appears to be scarce and this is especially true in the United States where individualism rules.

Since 2008, the velocity of money has been falling. However big the Wall Street numbers might be, the rate at which money changes hands within an economy or velocity of money is a better indicator of our lived experience of that flow. Money is being poured into the system now, only to be sucked up into financialization schemes betting on future profits down the line. Which brings us to betting schemes and crypto.

This is why the crypto world expands our sense of what money is and can do.

Various cryptocurrencies explore these dimensions of money: who can issue it, what it is backed by, whether it is useful to hoard it or spend it, if it can be attached to governance such as voting, and so much more.

Whether you are a fan of speculating or abhor the crazy dynamics, we can all admit it is reshaping our understanding of what is possible to operate as money.

In a way, the crypto world fills in a gap between store-issued gift certificates or coupons and government-issued currencies. It has and can create the experience of abundance.

Ethical Consequences

There are ethical consequences to our economic assumptions and tooling. Expressing value as a single-dimensional numeric value (like money does) can make it more difficult to consider ethical factors when weighing costs and benefits. It reduces our ability to make ethical comparisons, and it commoditizes humans.

This makes it easier to think about and solve many questions of production and distribution. A simple and well known example is the supply and demand function of labor, where it is deemed necessary for there to be some unemployment in the market as it functions to set the "fair" price of labor, and the individual toll on the humans involved is just accepted.

Virginie Glaenzer

Accounting Roots in Slavery

Did you know that our current and modern accounting system has roots in slavery[9]?

'*Accounting for Slavery*'[10] by Caitlin Rosenthal informs us about the complex relationships between slavery and capitalism. In her book, Rosenthal explores the development of quantitative management practices, sophisticated organizational structures, and an early form of scientific management. She describes how some people, *planters*, subjected others, *enslaved people*, to experiments. These pseudo-scientific experiments included allocating and reallocating labor from crop to crop, planning meals and lodging, and carefully recording daily productivity.

---

[9] https://www.marketplace.org/2018/08/14/disturbing-parallels-between-modern-accounting-business-slavery/

[10] https://www.hup.harvard.edu/catalog.php?isbn=9780674972094

From that time, planters depreciated their human capital decades before the practice was a widely used accounting technique.

The brutality of slavery was readily compatible with the development of new quantitative techniques for workforce organization.

Today, when your accountant writes off an asset to avoid paying taxes and your employees fill spreadsheets' rows and columns, they are performing tasks whose roots extend back to the era of slavery.

By examining the many ways that business innovation was a byproduct of slave labor, Rosenthal argues that capitalism and slavery were closely linked, revealing deep parallels between the outlooks of eighteenth- and nineteenth-century slaveholders and the ethical dilemmas facing twenty-first-century businesses.

Virginie Glaenzer

Power Money

<u>Today's economy is not just built on slavery but, more importantly, on power.</u>

For example, in Russia, it wasn't slavery exactly, it was serfdom. They too based their economic models and financial instruments on the backs of human suffering and war. The rise and fall of Empires can be traced by studying the transportation of grain. Historian Scott Reynolds Nelson and author of "Oceans of Grain", shows how the struggle to dominate grain-producing regions of the world transformed the balance of power, from ancient Rome to modern America: human suffering, money and debt instruments, and innovation. For example, he writes about Catherine the Great's need to appease the nobles of Russia and how that led to deeper oppression of the serfs there in a desire to create more wheat production. She created new financial instruments to fund a war with the Ottoman Empire so that Russia could establish control over a booming port in Odessa that acted as a lifeline for feeding wheat to much of Europe. After the US Civil War, more American wheat began flowing across the Atlantic, and food prices plummeted, which later became an important causal factor in the outbreak of the First World War and the Russian Revolution.

We cannot overlook how the United States and Russia, like other powerful nations, continue to use medieval practices based on supremacy consciousness in order to grab and maintain power relations.

It is such a challenge to get away from these approaches because of how deeply rooted it is within the system.

Virginie Glaenzer

Lost Relationships

Our society's heavy emphasis on monetized transactions has destroyed the relationships building inherent in the art of gift-giving. The erosion of the gift economy weakens the sense of belonging and trust in societies and leads to an increase in feelings of mistrust and alienation.

Giving to others builds bonds of trust and belonging and creates social fabric.

While economic theory assumes that people make rational choices, even most economists agree that the reality is quite different. Economic theory assumes that rational behavior drives human economic decision-making, but reality demonstrates how much humans make emotional decisions.

Making ethical choices in a village is possible.

But, in a global economy with all the abstraction and reduction to simplicity, it is a big challenge to engage in economic activity informed by personal values.

All that information about people's lived experiences, that we would know if we shared a village, gets erased by charts and graphs that focus on other aspects of the economy in dry numbers. And it isn't that charts and graphs themselves embody the issue, it is about the distance they create between people.

We can see the labels developing in the last few decades to help purchasers make more ethical decisions aligned with their values.

Conclusion

In conclusion, the growth persuasion mechanisms take advantage of human behavior by convincing people to buy things that aren't in their best interest nor sustainable. It doesn't even make the best products (as it promised), instead it pushes businesses to design for planned obsolescence, so more products can be sold again later.

This has gotten so far out of whack that, as a result, we are living under a form of oppression that forces students to live in debt and old people to continue working even after they have supposedly retired.

If our past economics were based on practices that we now see as unethical, can we then recognize how those tools perpetuate unethical behavior?

If we want different outcomes, what would upgrade the tools to fit those values?

There is another way forward.

CHAPTER TWO: WEALTH AND HEALTH

What if wealth is like health but for the social body?

We can now move from thinking about traditional economics to experiencing wealth differently. We even begin to see that wealth is not the same as accumulation.

The root of wealth is "weal" which means prosperity and well-being of the community.

What happens when we switch from individualistic hoarding and accumulation as a measure of personal wealth to better indicators of personal and community well-being and weal-being?

If you have actually made it through a disaster, you most likely learned that resilience turns out to be rooted in the people around us. <u>Historical data shows that, in times of crisis, people tend to help each other out.</u>

Distinguishing between Rival and Non-Rival

To clarify though, I am not suggesting that limits don't exist or that some things are not rare. Our emotional reaction to those limits or rarity trigger feelings of scarcity, a feeling manufactured to drive our desires for rare things.

Business schools teach that profitability comes from having more demand than supply.

By focusing on supply and demand, we have elevated the lived experience of scarcity as a driver for pricing.

The material world can display rarity, particularly in what is, in economic parlance, called "Rival Goods". For example, In *Limits to Growth*[11], they predicted we would run out of steel to make cars. Today vehicles simply use a lot less steel to be manufactured.

---

[11] https://en.wikipedia.org/wiki/The_Limits_to_Growth

<u>Today, we are experiencing a cornucopia of abundance: an abundance of information, education, ideas, services and experiences, global reach, access to expertise, investable wealth, and virtual experiences.</u>

These can be described as "Non-Rival" or "Partially-Rival" Goods in economics literature and they are particularly likely to be limited by artificial scarcity and enclosure. Releasing these from enclosure can increase our lived experience of abundance.

Partially Rival Goods like roads, internet access, and energy, benefit from tools that allow us to adjust our use based on availability. We can tune our energy consumption to better adapt to the availability of energy in the grid, for example. And people are innovating tools to help us do that.

Non-Rival Goods have often been made artificially scarce through enclosure: recipes, music, art, etc. Think about copyright as a way to enclose the flow of these. We see many innovations in the world today helping to support creators without creating enclosure. We can be patrons of creators and give social acknowledgement of their work.

Social and Technological Opportunities

This is an interesting moment ripe with possibility.

The internet and specifically the tradition of open source has inspired the growth of intelligent distributed organizations with less drive to create artificial scarcity through enclosure.

This is a game-changer for those who can see it. The information age gives birth to digital peer-to-peer networks and open knowledge.

New technologies continue to emerge, supporting drastically different ways of conducting business, as we have seen with technologies such as distributed ledger (including blockchain), the growth of machine learning and artificial intelligence (AI), and robotics.

Centralization and Decentralization

The Information Age arose, in large part, from an effort by central control.

It was, in part, inspired by an effort to avoid the risks of centralization. Road networks and the internet itself were designed to be resilient against nuclear attacks. We took those resilience patterns and have since recast them broadly.

Now, as these technologies mature, we have grown the ability to avoid centralized, hierarchical command-and-control mindsets.

To further live into this, we need new information and technology systems to understand and engage in this innovation wave.

CHAPTER THREE: REVISITING SCIENCE AND NATURE

To take advantage of this new wave, we may need to see from a different perspective.

We, humans, seem dedicated to innovation.

We often love to look to the natural world we are a part of to gain inspiration for our creativity. Humans are captivated by the many wonders that surround us and stimulated by the sight of the wild world's breathtaking beauty. And our sciences strive for a rigorous and objective way to make sense of how the natural world operates. It certainly got us this far.

But, over time we also recognize that our past innovations have faulty assumptions which seem to lead to some of the current undesirable outcomes.

For example, Economics, like many fields, borrowed from science in order to gain legitimacy in a world seeking greater rigor. It still runs on outdated science that has fallen into history books. Think of the difference between geocentrism and heliocentrism for a decent comparison of what we used to think and how science understands the solar system now.

Egocentric humans of the old version, put us at the center of the universe instead of seeing that the geometry reveals we are part of much vaster flows.

Economics may as well be based in the mythologies of alchemy at this point, the gap between the theory of rational actors and how humans actually are, turns out to be that vast.

<u>What happens to our economics if we update our views of the natural world using today's science? Does it change our understanding of how to approach economics? Does it enable abundance?</u>

Sadly, we might blame some of the errors of our old economics view on poor understandings of the past. And in the cases where the science might be right still, it may have been used in an unhelpful way.

For example, so much of the business "wisdom" from the 1980s and 90s seemed to come from a poor understanding of Darwin's evolutionary biology. Some of it is a trick of language, at least in English:

Does the survival of the *fittest* mean the *strongest* or the puzzle piece *fit*?

How did we get three-toed sloths and snails if the *fittest* means *strongest*?

And yet, the business world and economics focused on using this language of evolution to be an indicator of *progress* rather than of *change*. And it defined progress in terms of what is considered *stronger* or *better* from a human, subjective point of view.

This became a moral argument to justify why some succeed and others fail. Failing to thrive then becomes accepted as a moral consequence of weakness. Evolution rejects weakness. It is a twisted notion of a one-dimensional meritocracy.

In the wild world, we still find orchids and gazelles thriving rather than being replaced by the stronger dandelions and tigers.

Fittest really means *puzzle-piece-fit* and the ability to adapt to continue fitting as the ecology changes.

If those with the most power and influence can claim moral superiority for their dominance, it becomes easier to understand how we got to where we are now. Sit for a few hours in a meadow or forest and notice that the most common players in these ecosystems don't dominate the others; instead, they connect the system and contribute to it. They fit.

New Science and Other Ways of Knowing

If we are going to appeal to nature, then our models of nature would do well to better reflect our current understanding in the sciences. We may also benefit from allowing ourselves more ways of perceiving that world than just the western scientific methods.

Science shares a root word with scissors, and maybe we shouldn't just be cutting things up to understand them.

Unlike machines, living things and living systems tend to die when we cut them up and take them apart.

Still, it is worth considering where science has revealed new understandings, since economics likes to lean on it for rigor.

With Jean M. Russel's contribution[12], co-founder of Thrivable Society, I share five new developments in the field of science that may have you reevaluating your perceptions of the world around you. And these might provide clues about how we can engage in resource allocation that creates the lived experience of abundance for more people.

New Understanding of Genetics and HGT

Where does one species end and another begin?

Are the evolution of species even distinct lineages?

Darwin's depiction of species evolution didn't include the real complexity of what happens at the genomic level. We now know about horizontal gene transfer (HGT): that genes can cross species lines. This is described eloquently

---

[12] https://www.jeanmrussell.com/

in *The Tangled Tree: A Radical New History of Life* by David Quammen. Roughly eight percent of our own human genome came through viral infection, one type of HGT. Yep, through your DNA, you are part virus.

Consequently, we might all be a bunch more interdependent and interconnected than we thought we were.

If we are going to use evolution and genomics as a metaphor in economics, then maybe we need to consider interdependence and interconnection a bunch more. In the system science world, Gregory Bateson proposed that we consider the entity bee-flower rather than bee without flower, for example.

To apply these insights about identity and boundaries for individuation, we can ask, "How can we, and how do we borrow from the lessons others learn?" and "Where am I part of something else?"

Consider how something like Agile software

development methodology can be used by many organizations. This is like horizontal gene transfer. We don't each need to evolve on our own behind locked doors, we can learn from the adaptations others make.

This sharing of knowledge and practices has been bubbling up on the internet for years into a cultural expectation that information wants to be free.

New Understanding of Microbiology

Microbiology has revealed the depth of symbiosis throughout the living world. We often think of microbes as little horrors of disease, but they have been helping to direct our evolution all along. Catch up on this surprise with *I Contain Multitudes: The Microbes Within Us and a Grander View of Life* by Ed Yong.

Our microbiomes are a hidden force that defines our health, shapes our identities, and grants us abilities we could never imagine.

<u>Perhaps we may want to look at what microbes define our wealth and shape our sense of self?</u>

Think of it like this, we developed antibiotics because we seemed to think bacteria were bad, and some quite deadly. We could have been working *with* instead of *against* the critters because tons of them support our well-being. These days people talk more about probiotics and caring for the microbiome.

So what might you have viewed as needing extermination that actually has tons of benefits to offer in the right conditions?

Also, pushing to exterminate something may make it more resistant to control. So how do we work with it instead? What is the jiu jitsu move?

New Understanding of Fungus

Fungi have dashed onto the stage as more than food or molds. Fungi make up one of the five kingdoms of life, and their existence supports and gives life to almost everything else, including much of our plant life. Fungi can cure disease and even reverse environmental damage.

If the living world has an internet, it is made of fungi.

And the more we learn about fungi, the more it pushes up against our sense of what makes an individual and even what intelligence is.

To be inspired, read *Entangled Life: How Fungi Make Our Worlds, Change Our Minds & Shape Our Futures* by Merlin Sheldrake for more.

Taking in these updates in science, we could be inspired by how fungi handle supply chains, solve novel problems, and then we could worry less about individualism and focus more on participating in networks of reciprocity and abundance.

New Understanding of Forests

While the fungi networks play a significant role in most plant life, they serve more than one plant at a time. They connect plants to each other. **Forests, as a whole, turn out to be social cooperative super-creatures sharing nutrition and sensory awareness: trees warn their neighbors about bugs, disease, and fire.**

A slew of books covering this has hit the shelves, from *Finding the Mother Tree: Discovering the Wisdom of the Forest* by Suzanne Simard to the popular novel, *Overstory*.

Trees depend on each other, much as we do, and their community life is reminiscent of our own.

<u>In our cut-up science world, can we understand the value of the incredibly generous mother trees, feeding those around her? What can mother trees and forest ecosystems teach us about economic possibilities?</u>

In understanding forests, we left behind the short termism encapsulated in "get me mine" from Ayn Rand to find that mother nature more closely aligns greatness with responsibilities of care and cultivation for the long-term.

Where can we see the flows of support into and within networks and ecosystems and how can we create organizations that have reciprocity with such networks?

And Other Interesting Learnings about Humans

We haven't just changed our understanding of the science of microbiology or fungi or even plants, we also have shifted our understanding of how humans behave at many different layers. The book, *Behave: The Biology of Humans at Our Best and Worst* by Robert M. Sapolsky, starts at the moment of behavioral reaction and steps backward in time to reveal what had to happen for that reaction to occur.

What we eat, our hormones, our genetics, and our society all influence us and the actions we take.

It can be a bit terrifying to realize how something as simple as when a judge ate can influence their decisions in sentencing. Sending snacks if you want a good result might not just be a wild notion of good manners.

When we acknowledge all the factors that go into human decisions and behavior, the old world moral superiority of "strength" collapses completely.

So many of us read *Lord of the Flies* and felt anxious about this story of how humans supposedly are. In *Humankind*[13] Rutger Bregman tracks down the true-life story of boys castaway on an island. Turns out there wasn't anything so brutal as *Lord of the Flies* made us think.

---

[13] https://www.rutgerbregman.com/books

Actually, even pubescent boys can be generous with each other and work cooperatively. **Recent research is showing that late in human evolution Homo sapiens underwent a process of extreme selection for friendliness.**

That's right, humans tend toward cooperative behavior and seem to have self-domesticated. Read all about it in *Survival of the Friendliest*[14].

Maybe it would serve us well to look beyond science to other knowledge traditions such as indigenous knowledge, which you can get a glimpse of in books such as *"Braiding Sweetgrass"*[15] and *"Sand Talk"*[16] which weave between western knowledge and indigenous understanding.

---

[14] https://en.wikipedia.org/wiki/Survival_of_the_Friendliest

[15] https://milkweed.org/book/braiding-sweetgrass

[16] https://www.harpercollins.com/products/sand-talk-tyson-yunkaporta?variant=32280908103714

How Science Has Evolved

To pull it together then, here's the updated and more accurate story.

<u>Humans turn out to be highly cooperative creatures with a strong need for reciprocity and to be a contribution (have a purpose). The line between us and other creatures tends to be blurry.</u>

Individualism might even be a convenient illusion we hold on to.

Humans are deeply enmeshed with life. Much of our bodies aren't even human cells, and even some of our genes aren't human. Rather than focusing on what makes one species survive or not, maybe the whole thing is a bit more of a cooperation game: an upward spiral[17] of life supporting life to creating more life.

---

[17] Paul Krafel https://www.youtube.com/watch?v=5thxvIdEds4

And if we want to take some wisdom from the wild world on how to live through challenging experiences, maybe the fungus and trees have lessons for us in communicating and contributing.

The wild world seems less about rational, self-interested unfeeling automatons and more purpose-driven, friendly, cooperation.

Most of Life Happens in Cooperation

Jean M Russel[18], founder of the thrivability movement, offers a new way of looking at the competition versus cooperation.

The old ways of thinking twisted Darwin's idea about evolution to focus on brutal competition, but somehow that doesn't quite explain the long term existence of the three-toed sloth, butterflies, or sea slugs.

---

[18] https://www.jeanmrussell.com/

Competition might be where the sizzle happens, the friction and sense of victory we sometimes yearn for, but we hyperfocus on it at our own expense.

Besides, we can't compete in sports without first cooperating on the rules of the game.

<u>Most of life happens in cooperation.</u> Humans are deeply wired for cooperation. We long for connection and are strongly influenced by each other.[19] This isn't a weakness. It is our greatest strength and resilience. It is even how we out-innovated those humanoids that were physically stronger than us: band together and skill-share.

Take off the competition framing and see cooperation. For example, most drivers aren't competing for the road most of the time, most people can pass by or interact with others in broadly trusting ways.

---

[19] Cialdini's work on Persuasion
https://www.goodreads.com/book/show/28815.Influence

It is a bit of wonder that our business plans focus on Competitive Analysis rather than Cooperative Analysis[20].

Case Study

A transportation logistics team explored carbon reductions. Through their analysis, they discovered that multiple publishing houses were shipping books to the same stores using different trucks. The publishing houses could reduce transit costs and carbon emissions by coordinating transport together to the stores.

The publishing houses resisted at first because they saw themselves as competitors. When reminded of their unique value and that it did not have anything, even remotely, to do with the transit of their goods, and that they could both save money; then they were able to see

---

[20] https://medium.com/@nurturegirl/competition-analysis-why-not-cooperation-analysis-bcd9c81ca64d

their way to collaborate on delivery to bookstores. Fewer carbon emissions, more financial efficiency, and nobody sacrificing their unique value.

After all, it is who is helping you succeed that has a much greater bearing on whether you do indeed succeed than anything your competitors do[21].

For many of us, cooperation is 95% of our experience, yet we focus on the 5% that isn't working or feels full of competition and friction. The drama of it.

Or to be less binary about it, most of our experiences tend to be mostly cooperative most of the time. Maybe if we focus on doing more of what works, we might get more of it.

---

[21] https://pollinate.net/organizational-ecosystem-engagement

Cooperation Analysis

Try doing a cooperation analysis by making a list of all the ways people have cooperated with you this week.

<u>Do you notice more of what works or what does not?</u>

Include cooperation such as following the rules while walking and driving in such a way as to not damage your person or your vehicle. How many transactions have you done that went smoothly?

Similarly then, what might happen if we focused on the relationships that make us more likely to be successful rather than the ones we are trying to compete against?

We suspect anyone who has been shoulder to shoulder with others during a disaster learns that resilience and agility are stored in the relationships around us.

Look at who you and your organization engage with.

1. Where are your MOUs (Memorandum of understanding)?
2. Who else is striving for similar impact or regulation in your industry?
3. Who can you ally with on anything that isn't your unique value proposition?
4. Who else might be aligned with your purpose that you could mutually benefit from an alliance with?
5. Who are your biggest supporters?
6. Who champions your vision and brand best?

Several years ago, before the pandemic, Nilofer Merchant and others, started talking about the Social Era[22]: *"Smart companies are letting social become the backbone of their business models, increasing their speed and flexibility by pursuing openness and fluidity."*

Let's focus on the ecosystem.

> How can we work like a whole meadow or forest together?
>
> Who acts like the trees creating the canopy, and who is the moss?
>
> What is the mycelium under the forest floor facilitating the communication between many of the species thriving in the forest?
>
> How do we take the openness and fluidity that Merchant argues for and connect with others?

<u>You can only be as successful as those you depend on.</u>

What are you doing to increase cooperation with your upstream and downstream dependencies? Who else can be cultured for future cooperation?

---

[22] https://nilofermerchant.com/big-ideas/socialera/

Do a cooperative analysis and be sure to include all the parties you depend on and all who depend on your cooperation.

You might be surprised by what you have to offer that others can benefit from. And others might surprise you with their generosity when everyone is clear about their own value proposition as a cooperator within the ecosystem.

CHAPTER FOUR: WHAT IS ABUNDANCE?

In this book, we are challenging the meta-narrative running the show: scarcity.

However, when I'm talking about abundance, I am not talking about abundance as a very large quantity of something.

In the "Abundance Economy", abundance means not having more than what we need.

I define abundance as having *enough when needed*.

Therefore, to live in a state of abundance requires us to swim in possibilities and opportunities—passing over what we think we "need" and choosing what we truly want—and then letting them go into our own bodies, minds, and wills. The experience of abundance is less than plenty and more than sufficient.

To thrive in abundance, we need to find balance and stand in our own center to resist being pushed or pulled by external forces.

Finding that space to stand in our center—where we can see and act on our own values—can help us resist the pull of others' expectations and the fear mongers at large.

<u>We can start by asking ourselves a very personal question; how much is enough?</u>

The Layers of Abundance

Abundance is not one thing, it's many things.

It's an understanding, a perspective, a feeling and, finally a practical way of living.

Understanding

First, today's economy is not just in a recession with disrupted supply chains or inflation: it's the end of an era. We are finding ourselves at the emergence of intelligent distributed organizations. This is a game-changer for those who can see it.

What I'm bringing to light is that the information age that has given birth to digital peer-to-peer networks and open knowledge. As a result, barriers to industries, shareholder investment thresholds, and geographies have fallen. That has created an abundance of ideas, tools, knowledge, people, opportunities.

A few new phenomena are making the invisible abundance visible:

1. Technologies of peer networks are enabling an abundance of relationships
2. Open source is making knowledge available to most

<u>There is plentiful technology, plentiful information, plentiful compute power, plentiful money, and plentiful human energy and ideas in our world.</u>

Secondly, our sense of self is wrongly a feeling of individuality because in reality, the individuality doesn't really exists. We are a collection of events, actions, memory, thoughts, and ideas. We're all our ancestors and ourselves at the same time. We are abundance in a way.

Thirdly, abundance is linked to our craving for independent which has cut off our relationships but relationships are what brings meaning and abundance. The western view of the concept of individuality and the American dream was built on the idea of independence and becoming self-sufficient. But this deprived us from relationships which is where we found meaning and abundance.

Perspective

History is a story told by the winners and rewritten in books. So scarcity is just another story told to us. Scarcity is created and manufactured by greed. As an example, our concept of Intellectual Property illustrates how our economic system struggles to deal with the abundance of information. While the value of information tends to increase with greater sharing, businesses often try to limit access to that information, creating an artificial scarcity. However, the value of information tends to increase the more it is shared, highlighting the disconnect between our economic system and the fundamental nature of information.

I invite you to ask yourself what are the other areas manufactured by scarcity.

Feeling

To live a beautiful life is one where not everything can be based on transaction, for profit or consumption. I just know deep down that life is not about consuming, extracting, and protecting at all costs. I hold firmly in my bones the belief that there is enough for everyone on this planet.

Practical Way of Living

If scarcity stems from a fear of lacking due to our desire for independence, and leads to hoarding, then abundance can be viewed as a vast buffet of abundance. In order to access this abundance, we are asked to reflect on our past experiences with scarcity.

The case study in chapter one describes how being clear about your uniqueness and value proposition makes you feel centered and allows you to flow with others. This gives us time to pursue what's important to us rather than trying to keep up with everyone else.

Abundance is everywhere in our society but invisible to those whose worldview is not open to seeing anew.

The challenge for most people is to understand how the believing in scarcity gives rise to the idea of competition. When we focus on our competitors, we become fearful and try to win at all costs.

Conversely, when we focus on our own needs and desires for cooperation, we create lasting connections with others based on shared values.

Nonrival goods can be used by one consumer without decreasing their supply to another consumer. An example of a nonrival good is a recipe, for say, apple pie. The recipe can be used to make apple pie. It can be shared and those people can also make apple pie. The recipe doesn't decrease for having been used to make apple pie multiple times. It isn't consumed.

Other examples of this are musical performances and broadcast songs. A partially-rival good is one that can be used by one individual without seeming to diminish the amount available to others, but when the sum of use exceeds availability, access diminishes; examples include electricity and roads (think of traffic backing up when it hits a threshold of use).

That brings us to the question, how do we experience wealth?

Principles of abundance on a finite planet

How do we organize to take advantage of this abundance so everyone has elegant sufficiency?

And how do we replace our systems without removing the positives that previous generations achieved through ordered society?

Not all of us have the same opportunities, yet almost all the new emerging technologies create huge value. It is important to share the wealth by taking advantage of these new paradigms to unleash real solutions for people and companies alike.

Before Scarcity	After Abundance
Mindset: Control and competition to resist uncertainty. Focus on self-interest. Ownership.	**Mindset**: Openness to emergence for possibilities and collaboration. Focus on the health of the system. Access.
Process: Extraction	**Process**: Cultivation

and accumulation.	and care.
Resource: Labor intensive, and cogs in the machine.	**Resource**: Technology enhanced and organic, human-centered design.

The worldwide pandemic has changed so much of our world. We can't hide things under the rug anymore. The just-in-time world ended with supply-chain failures and changing border conditions.

New values have emerged along with the acceptance of a new reality: climate change has become more visible through fires and droughts and the enormous toll of emotional labor has brought forward the need for emotional well-being.

Virginie Glaenzer

There is a global movement of organizations, platforms, and people all trying to serve the creation of a more beautiful world. They do it by bringing together four specific pieces of a puzzle. These pieces form any living ecosystem: life giving rise to more life, community of relationships, governance otherwise known as feedback loops, and creativity.

To build a new economy, each of those pieces is being rewritten:

1. **Values**: Abundance value is a set of beliefs. Equity, inclusion, and respect for nature which in time create a new society's culture.

2. **Community**: we no longer want to be told what to do and be part of hierarchical organizations. We want our voice to be heard in community. A group will develop open relationships from a proposal of shared values, purpose, place, or practice.

3. **Governance**: Our new culture and our desire for communities show up in how we want to be led and lead others. We move away from centralization and trading off agency for supposed efficiency and towards distributed, fluid structures of connecting. We're seeing steward ownership, workers' coops, multi-stakeholder co-operatives, b-corps, and other forms of decentralized leadership structures empowering a sense of inclusion and belonging with more transparency and trustworthy systems.

4. **Technology:** Creativity by way of Technology is the last piece to complete this puzzle. New types of infrastructure are emerging, enabling these communities and new forms of governance to become a reality, transcending prior limitations of location or knowledge management.

CHAPTER FIVE: THE NEW ECONOMY

The Business of Abundance

Let's look at how abundance thinking works.

Leadership models have been closely tied to our industrial needs, reflecting the mindset of leaders and the assumptions they made at the time.

According to Prof. Julian Birkinshaw[23] from the London Business School, we have witnessed how *"the sources of competitive advantage are changing, from the industrial era to the knowledge era to the post-knowledge era"*, which he describes as the Hand, the Head, and the Heart.

---

[23] https://www.youtube.com/watch?v=UeQkmYJFIhw

During the industrial revolution, manual labor was a priority, and managers just needed bodies to get the work done. This Hand phase saw managers leading with an iron fist, forcing their workers to do the work, and that work mostly involved what the worker's hands did. Micromanagement was commonplace during this era. We focused on physical limits.

The information revolution, known as the Head phase, was the data and knowledge phase. During this time, the more knowledge a person had, the more valuable they became. Management focuses on inviting workers to think about work whenever possible. Controlling hands isn't helpful for knowledge work. Companies wanted intelligence because Information was capital. We test the edges of intellectual limits.

Today, the business world is moving towards the Heart phase, where leaders must be emotionally intelligent to adapt and navigate complex social situations.

Virginie Glaenzer

Management focuses on inspiration and passion for engaging people in their purpose. As a society, we are exploring the landscape of emotions (feelings that create motion, *e-motion*).

Once we shift into passion and purpose, people can throw off the shackles of management to choose to align together to achieve shared goals.

<u>We see the emergence of social technologies to enable collaborations for a shared purpose.</u>

This shift is enabled on multiple fronts.

Some of this change comes from legal innovations, creating social technologies that enable groups of people to form entities with shared ownership across state boundaries and beyond the limits of traditional banking. These newer legal forms shift the dynamics of groups, encouraging contribution and risk taking by those involved.

This also comes from innovations in funding methods, from crowdfunding to ICOs/tokenomics, which brings the participants along in the development of the entity and products. Again, this reduces risk by sharing it and aligns emotional energy with effort and investment.

We have innovations in logistics, increasing efficiencies of flows within ecosystems, not just within organizations. To cooperate in ecosystems, we have to get beyond the defensive boundary behaviors of competitive efficiency efforts and switch into seeking shared gains.

Finally, we have innovations in automation, continuing to hand off to robots and computers/the internet many of the things which can be standardized or tend towards repetitiveness.

In 2016, this evolution gave rise to decentralized autonomous organizations (DAO) which require trust in the tools to temper against the difficulty of trusting anonymous others.

A decentralized autonomous organization (DAO), sometimes called a decentralized autonomous corporation (DAC) is an organization represented by rules encoded as a transparent computer program, controlled by the organization members, and not influenced by a central government[24]. In other words, DAOs are member-owned communities without centralized leadership.

---

[24] Wikipedia:
https://en.wikipedia.org/wiki/Decentralized_autonomous_organization

Virginie Glaenzer

The old era of business created KPIs that reinforced scarcity which leads to more scarcity. In the workplace, KPIs often focus on individual zero-sum games and hold people accountable for individual actions. <u>But we need shared game goals and indicators that reflect those shared aspirations.</u>

This form of abundant business is an invitation to choose new key indicator performances (KPIs) driving business growth that will put people above the economy, and for a company to prioritize its people (ability to keep evolving) over its profits (ability for executives to take bonuses).

Virginie Glaenzer

What Business Models Can We Learn From Nature?

Many technologies were inspired and borrowed their designs from nature; flight, submarines, velcro, bullet trains, and sonar, just to name a few. Humans look at living systems and design amazing creations advancing humanity's progress.

<u>What if we would look at nature once again to design the next generation of business models?</u>

Could we be able to go beyond the Blue Ocean Strategy[25] model into new systems where we experience something we could name *Green Pastures and unleash Meadow Systems*?

An important living system process is called symbiosis.

---

[25] The Blue Ocean Strategy: www.blueoceanstrategy.com/what-is-blue-ocean-strategy

Symbiosis is the interaction between two different organisms living in close physical association, typically to the advantage of both. Symbiosis is also a mutually beneficial relationship between different people or groups.

<u>What if we changed our relationships from competition built into our current economic models to symbiotic ones?</u>

Nilofer Merchant, an author ranked by Thinkers50 as one of the world's leading thinkers, shares a radical understanding: *"Existing business models were predicated on making things (products, services) vs. connecting things (what the fundamental shift is with internet models). It's not that we won't keep making things from products (hotels, cars, servers) but that the ability to monetize ideas is not tied to a thing anymore."*

In light of this new worldview, it is safe to say that the cost of production is no longer the core requirement for payment models and resource flows. We used to say that the product cost X to produce, up it by a margin, and charge the buyer that total as the price of goods. Pricing has become unhinged from costs of production.

Today, we have lots of ways to make only some of the people pay a premium, and lots of people can then be subsidized to use at least a base version, designing mutually beneficial relationships between different people or groups.

In our current economy, for a business to thrive, it needs the income to exceed the expenses and provide a return on any capital invested in it. If this is not working, it needs to either increase income or decrease expenses, or project such a change in the future. This is a cash flow game, once there is a functioning product or service at hand.

I will not go into qualities of functioning product or service, I will presume for purposes here, that there is a functional product or service. Let's consider, as an example, one of the business models of the internet today: **advertising**.

The current advertising business models has these upsides:

> Advertising subsidizes use by participants who are not paying and enables large scale (volume) of small scale (intimate) interactions - billions of people sharing in small groups and communities. (Check out any recipe blog, for instance)
>
> It begins to build toward collective intelligence in participants (bakers, for instance).
>
> But it also has major downsides:
>
> The selling of data and bombarding the community with advertisements.

This is the model most troubling, as the incentives in the model drive the platform (social media) to service advertisers and data clients (usually the same thing) rather than the "users" because the "users" are the product, not the purchaser. That might not be too horrific until we see the impacts - Cambridge Analytica and the Russian influence on the election of Trump.

Another business model of the internet today is **freemium services.**

Some small sets of "users" pay for premium services while some larger sets of "users" are subsidized, gaining free services. In a sense, the freemium model has moved away from advertising because the community of participants IS the funnel toward premium payments, if designed well.

Both of these approaches have been a gateway between the "cost of production" pricing model and the accessibility to technology and information today.

Where is this taking us? What comes next for abundance approaches?

The New Economy Of Abundance

Abundance is all around us if we look for it.

We have the resources we need around us to thrive. The only reason we don't understand how to tap into this abundance is that we have been conditioned to believe in scarcity to drive price and purchasing, even where scarcity doesn't really exist.

The truth is that abundance surrounds us, waiting to be tapped into freely.

Here are three ways business abundance is manifesting.

Virginie Glaenzer

Abundance Technology

The technology revolution is all about abundance.

Today, we create and share content, find and connect with people, and use technology to do more in less time. But the technology revolution isn't just about an abundance of tools. It's also about an abundance of data. The price of data storage has dropped by over 90% in the last 10 years alone.

This revolution has driven a new era of digital music that benefits both fans and artists. Today, two billion people around the world enjoy the benefits of streaming music on the platforms they know and love. And artists have never had more ways to connect with fans through social media, videos, live events, and other innovative tools. It's helping them build careers, find new audiences, and make money from their art.

In addition, the power of Blockchain, AI, and Automation innovations lies in their ability to make the most scarce resource of all abundant: time.

These technologies continue the pattern of technology being deployed on repetitive tasks and extend that into the dimensions of more refined physical work and physical work at a distance in the case of robotics, analysis of data in the case of AI and automating contracts as code in the case of blockchain.

Some associate this increased efficiency with the precarity of work (jobs replaced by machines), however, from an abundance point of view, freeing up our most scare resource, time, to be able to redirect it toward passion and purpose comes as a gift.

And the precarity can be addressed through technology for social networks with broader social fabric to support mutual aid networks and access to meaningful work.

Offering new possibilities for people to build relationships and co-create like never before, decentralized organizations and remote work make elegant sufficiency more possible.

This abundant access to expertise & knowledge combined with global reach can be a power for good.

Funding Abundance: Crowd Platforms

The crowd is the new frontier and crowd platforms are becoming the new marketplace opportunities. Crowd platforms are the most disruptive innovation in business and commerce since the Internet. They combine the cloud, mobile, social media, AI, and blockchain technologies. They enable small businesses to tap into underserved markets that were previously too expensive or complex to enter.

Investing can be a game-changer for many people. As laws and regulations adapt to new securities, new opportunities arise.

As an example, Wefunder uses a provision in the 2012 JOBS Act which allows unaccredited investors to purchase equity in early stage private companies. StartEngine uses Regulation A+ according to which a non-accredited investor can only invest a maximum of 10% of their annual income or 10% of their net worth per year, whichever is greater.

Other platforms startups are using are SeedInvest Technology or Equitybee, while Nonprofits connect on MightyCause.

Abundance through crowd platforms can also apply for creative professionals with Patreon or for individuals with GoFundMe.

This trend of massively cooperative businesses with abundance rooted in their DNA can lead to innovating brands that deeply understand the importance of communities built within. Communities create in fundamentally different ways than traditional organizations built on the belief of scarcity. Empowering a community requires the understanding that the community is not yours alone and that requires a conscience letting go of control, which is another example of leading from the heart.

In the abundance economy, people have the ability to use existing resources to create something new through the process of mixing, or combining, transforming, and copying these resources. This allows individuals and communities to innovate and contribute to the co-creation of new ideas and solutions.

This process called Remix[26] invites individuals and communities to participate in the innovation process and foster a diverse range of ideas and approaches by copying, transforming, and combining to create something new.

Overall, the abundance economy is an exciting new model that has the potential to revolutionize the way we live, work, and create. It empowers individuals and communities to take charge of their own innovation and to participate in the co-creation of new ideas and solutions.

Crowd platforms are an adaptive form of creation that pushes forward information and ideas into abundant wealth of knowledge.

Investable Wealth Abundance

If the accumulation of personal wealth and the sharing of collective resources were mutually reinforcing activities, what would that look like?

---

[26] https://www.youtube.com/watch?v=MZ2GuvUWaP8

One of the most fundamental requirements of a capitalist economic system—and one of the most sacred cow concepts—is *own*ership.

An abundance economy comes, in part, from giving people *access*. This encourages people to invest in physical and human capital, as well as technology for broader benefit than the individual. The hidden cost of ownership is the maintenance thereof, and many are appreciating the ability to have access without the burden of upkeep and improvement. The sharing economy has given us insight into how to access together without ownership, and where we have ownership to benefit from sharing access.

In the same way, giving employees, customers, partners, and anyone involved in a company's growth, access to capital ownership is going to not only revolutionize the future of fundraising but will also build the abundance economy, powered by digital ledger accounting and smart contract technologies.

This is the employee compensation redefined - wages plus dividends already lives in many crypto projects.

Once the domain of high wealth and privilege, we are now witnessing the rise of co-ownership with much lower barriers to entry.

The rise of alternative investing, from NFT ownership to private equity funds, represents investable wealth abundance.

Everyone is a shareholder in something, with Robinhood slice of shares to Angellist slide of start-ups, the micro-everything removes barriers to entry.

Another example of investable wealth abundance are organizations whose mission is to spread economic opportunity more equitably around the world. Braintrust[27] is a decentralized talent network — one that is user-owned removing middlemen redistributing value in a more fair way to talent and organizations.

Pushing this trend even further, I imagine a new abundance economy, evolving us from a Centralized Hierarchical Welfare State towards distributed community-engaged micro investors and federated abundance economies.

Rather than the state giving "hand-to-mouth" welfare to those falling through the cracks of extractive capitalist machinery, imagine that there is an additional opportunity for anyone to fund and/or invest in individuals or shares of communities and companies to self-sustain livelihood through micro-opportunities. Mutual Aid blurring into investment strategies.

Wealth takes many shapes and forms.

---

[27] https://www.usebraintrust.com/

Wealth expresses itself from market value (Financial Wealth), status (Social Wealth), freedom (Time Wealth), to health (Physical Wealth). Therefore, it's important to rethink abundance in wealth to uncover what is still invisible and make it visible.

In conclusion, finding business abundance means focusing on the freedom of minds and letting go of some of our limiting beliefs that hinder prosperity.

Social innovation happens when we connect people with unmet needs to people with spare capacity.

Virginie Glaenzer

CHAPTER SIX: THE ABUNDANT FRAMEWORK

The Abundance Innovation Framework

Eight New Business Areas to build an Abundance Organization in the 21st Century

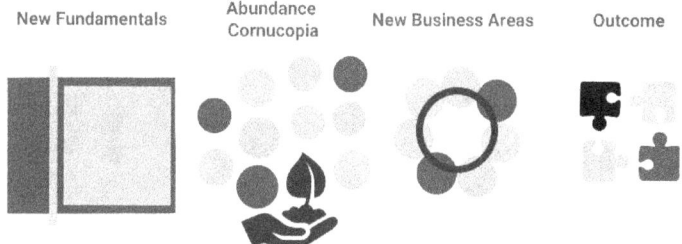

New Fundamentals   Abundance Cornucopia   New Business Areas   Outcome

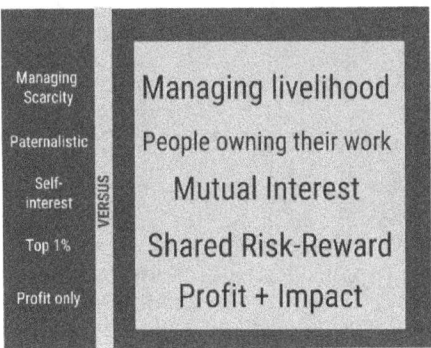

New Economy Fundamentals

"The Abundance Economy" describes how the role of economics is to create livelihoods instead of managing scarcity.

I describe how economics has been a management science that focused on the optimal allocation of limited resources (a.k.a. "scarcity management") rather than on production and allocation.

I invite people to better engage with their livelihood and move away from the current reliance on paternalistic institutions.

The abundance economy distributes power and functionality among all who contribute, encouraging a cooperative community by providing a risk and rewards mechanism for the contributors, based on the value of their contributions, the sharing of risk, and the amount at stake.

Finally, this new economic approach embraces the alchemy of Profit+Impact *versus* profit only, cultivating *versus* extraction, and mutual interests *versus* self-interest.

Virginie Glaenzer

A Cornucopia of Abundance

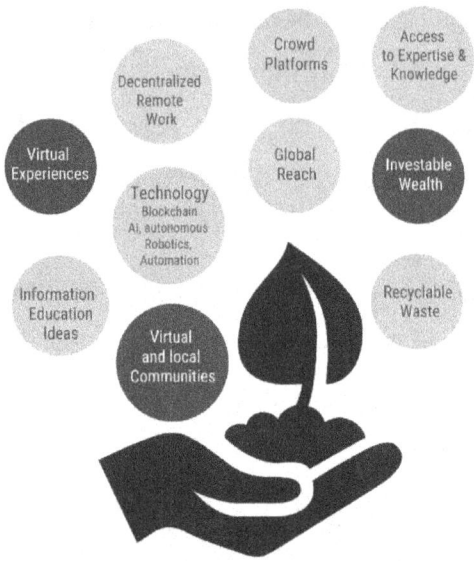

When we adopt the worldview of abundance, a cornucopia of possibilities and tools becomes available to us.

These possibilities emerge from the following areas:

Technologies (Blockchain/ AI & autonomous/ Robotics & Automation)

Decentralized and remote work

Access to expertise & knowledge

Crowd-platforms

Information

Education

Global reach

Recyclable waste

Investable wealth

Virtual and local communities and virtual experiences.

Virginie Glaenzer

New Business Outcomes Unleashed

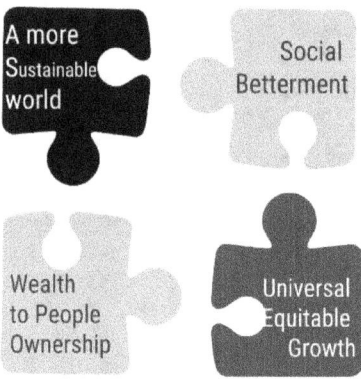

This new worldview leads to a more abundant world by promoting employee and participatory ownership in a cooperative, shareholder-driven economy rather than state-driven capitalism.

It blurs class boundaries and increases democratic engagement.

As a result, this opportunity from government handout to community investment can result in social betterment and universal equitable growth.

Virginie Glaenzer

Eight Circles Of Abundance

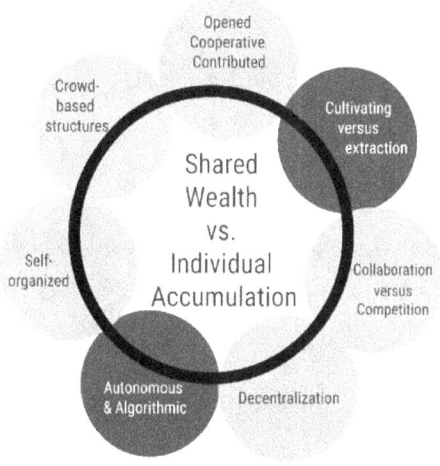

I am presenting eight circles of abundance that will empower abundance to emerge and help the new organization of the twenty-first century succeed.

These circles of abundance are essential to the emergence of abundance-based organizations.

1. Opened, Cooperative & Contributed

In the age of abundance, employees require a sense of motivation and passion to perform their best. To tap into this potential, organizations are creating new cultures and leadership strategies that foster employee participation as valued members to the organization. Many companies now find ways of having employees self-organize and self-manage.

Zappos engaged and evolved their use of Holocracy[28].

Morning Star offers another case study in self-management[29].

---

[28] https://www.zapposinsights.com/about/holacracy

[29] https://corporate-rebels.com/morning-star/

As an example, profit-sharing distribution plans ensure that employees participate as valued members of the organization. When facing challenging business problems like budget cuts or layoffs, some organizations sell the business to the employees creating a Cooperative.

In this shifted structure, it is more possible to get the internal alignment for everyone to give up a little to keep the whole afloat. Cooperative structures are good at facing these challenging decisions with group collaboration, doing things a top down organization could not. Lighter weight versions of this method include profit-sharing.

2. Shared Wealth vs. Individual Accumulation

The new abundant organization is redefining employee compensation because when everything is reduced to money, then money becomes a constraint in the system and challenges viability.

If we can look at other forms of capital available, we might manage different cash flows. When we make visible our shared wealth and place it in relationship with individual motivation rather than individual accumulation, new forms of shared wealth appear.

Of course nonprofits have been doing this for some time, acknowledging in-kind contributions as one of the forms of contribution they receive. We can also see efforts to track and acknowledge sweat equity even if direct compensation doesn't happen at the time of effort.

As social network science continues to reveal, the networks of referrals we give, connecting people who can bring their contributions, paid, discounted, or in-kind also act as a form of wealth sharing.

That social wealth and brand wealth can be leveraged. Time wealth can be redirected. It's important to ask what counts and how things are counted to understand what is valued and how it flows.

3. Autonomous & Algorithmic

As we increase our connections to others, we can augment those relationships with technologies. Sorting through information and noise is something machines can do more effectively than we can. Think of how spreadsheets have assisted with accounting. Now, thanks to smart contracts, we can have improvements made to the inter-organizational space and administrative tasks delivered.

Flickr had a small percentage of headcount compared to Kodak. Instagram might be even lower head count, as it engages it even more at the community and ecosystem level with the secret sauce in the algorithms that drive visibility.

Additionally, the protocols for central banks and the limits of international legal structures have challenged our ability to work as international collectives.

In the old era, working across national boundaries with bank accounts was an administrative nightmare or challenged jurisdictional law. The new DAOs allow groups to form across jurisdictions and act as an organization together under their own governance agreements (or the jurisdiction of the DAO).

Composability and shifts in authority are two important factors that contribute to the emergence of self-organized structures. This is giving rise to Web3 embedding a new way to distribute and exchange value, unconstrained by legacy financial infrastructure. It is risky but exciting.

Today, almost every aspect of banking, lending and trading is managed by centralized systems. Regular consumers need to deal with middlemen to get an auto loan, a mortgage, trading stocks and bonds. DEFI, made possible by blockchain, is a brand new monetary system to empower users, by offering an alternative to the old and outdated traditional financial system, or by providing access where it is lacking.

It challenges this centralized financial system by disempowering middlemen and gatekeepers, and empowering everyday people via peer-to-peer exchanges.

4. Self-Organized Structures

The new organization is self-organized.

It's based on creating consent and alignment about how the process works, so each of the humans engaged can get what they need and have meaningful encounters with others.

This is about going beyond collaborative projects and learning how a self-organized and fluid hierarchy, or decision-making process assemblage, can empower teams to weave disparate elements in order to come up with novel solutions.

This approach to decision-making moves teams beyond Agile to the next level of Altshuller's[30] structure of inventive problem solving, where a self-organized and fluid hierarchy enables team members to assemble non-related elements as they see fit, unlocking creativity.

---

[30] https://en.wikipedia.org/wiki/TRIZ

5. Decentralized Organization

After a long phase of striving for efficiencies of scale, many of us have realized that some of the inefficiencies came from scaling itself.

The approaches for scaling relied on centralization, which increased the distance and reduced the flows between the edges of experience and the heart of decision-making and power. Learning cycles and information feedback loops in these structures were not as efficient or rapid as much more decentralized efforts, which becomes increasingly important in an accelerating world.

So we find ourselves, strangely now using decentralizing as a strategy for adaptation. Decentralizing through remote work has become an increasingly popular practice in the workplace. What happens in the absence of a chain of command?

With the great resignation of traditional employment a reality, work independence and self-determination are the biggest motivators for shaping the future of work.

Today, freelancing, remote working, and fractional work offer people the ability to move in and out of organizations freely. Organizational efficiency can be improved with "just-in-time" workers, as long as precarity of those workers isn't a blocker and passion/shared purpose form an attractor for the work to be done.

Remote and fractional resources fundamentally are changing the way we think of resources and require new trust and collaboration tools and processes to succeed.

Post-COVID, more companies are experimenting with alternative work schedules and the four-day workweek is becoming a trend among many organizations.

Virginie Glaenzer

Command and control leadership models are evolving into a new form of cooperation that involves sharing some of the decision-making with those participating in getting the work done.

6. Crowd-based Structures

The economics of abundance ultimately leads to crowdsourcing. Micro-task crowdsourcing—which involves people performing small tasks for pay—has become more common. For instance, when millions of people logged in to reCAPTCHA to translate nonsensical words into text, they were actually helping digitize old books and newspapers for free.

New product innovation links directly to the economics of abundance too. Kickstarter and other crowdfunding platforms offer plentiful examples of companies enabling swarms of people to pledge community support for innovative projects.

Crowdsourcing has also had a profound effect on the investment markets. On Wefunder, for example, everyone from mom-and-pop retail investors to Silicon Valley venture capitalists can invest in companies.

Crowd solutions bring a large number of people to contribute small bits (money, time, skill and other forms of capital) to efforts that previously had been done by few with more to contribute. Basically this is about math. 1 person gives $100 or 100 people give $1, same total. But way more people (more than 100x) can contribute $1, so goals become more accessible if the technology makes it easy and reliable to do so.

7. Collaboration versus competitions

The abundant organization challenges the idea of competition and instead explores ways to collaborate with people through shared purpose. Leading organizations only compete against themselves. Everyone else seems to think they have to compete with the best rather than defining themselves as having their own space, core value, and partners.

Organizations that bring out more collaboration in their ecosystem create a market advantage that comes from everyone working toward a shared goal.

"We need to imagine the fundamental enterprise anew for the social era. Lean, adaptive, community-driven organizations, built for speed, will thrive." Nilofer Merchant[31]

8. Cultivating Versus Extraction

Tons of people strive to create a more circular economy by repurposing waste from one into inputs for another so that the resources we need are not depleted. In parallel, relocalizing efforts strive to create circular economies where produce grown locally can be processed and sold locally, reducing the risk of long distance transport and keeping money in the local economy.

---

[31] https://hbr.org/2012/02/rules-for-the-social-era

New business opportunities include companies that mine recyclable goods, which can be used in new products, and hyperlocal businesses, which serve communities and reduce the need for transportation. As a result, communities can be made more self-sustaining with hyperlocal systems.

If we cultivate people and push ideas into the commons rather than enclosing spaces, then we get more of an experience of abundance and less of an experience of instrumentalist extraction.

Abundance Approach

Tribal Leadership[32] revealed four basic mindsets that were shared by group members:

1. Not enough, get mine or die
2. Not enough to share, uncooperative
3. Enough for us to share, cooperative

---

[32] https://www.triballeadership.net/

4.   Enough for everyone, generous

Which of these mindsets appeals to you?

When you choose your mindset, you become the world you want to live in by making different choices. What is possible when we come from *"There is enough to share"*, and are either generous or at least cooperative?

Even if you just want to use your capital effectively or maximize your income, an abundance approach makes sense. It is much more financially viable to give away some of what we create in order to market that thing. That might seem counter-intuitive, but if you use marketing budget to encourage people to test and play with what is valuable this turns out to have high returns that customers welcome.

Forms of "Resource" for the Cash Flow Game

When you zoom out from these business innovations, there are some patterns worth noticing. An important aspect of the abundant economy resides in the fact that not everything has to move through money.

There are various forms of payment or types of resources to be engaged in the *'cash flow'* game, as long as the input of the resource meets the needs of the organization, it is okay to skip "money" as an intermediary in the flow.

In the economics of abundance, an Economics of Flows starts to emerge.

These usage of resources vary in appropriateness based on the dynamics of the business involved. What will work for software, where the addition of users beyond a certain threshold is basically free, will have different characteristics than an apple farm, where the number of apples produced is finite and you need to optimize around perishability too. What works in one phase of a product or organization for the financial model may not be well suited for the next phase.

In general, the phases might be something like the initial fundraising - startup phase, scaling/refining phase, and maturing phase.

For example, when a project gets off the ground, a lot of social capital can help get it started. But as the organization scales, it needs to start getting more fungible resources to ease scaling costs.

Consider these flows to manage resources:

1. **Money:** obviously, and various forms of currency act like money (gift certificates, miles, etc.) If short on funds, consider other monetary tools like loyalty points and play with time as CSAs and gift certificates do.

2. **Time:** Not only can you create agreements about the time gap between payment and service/product, you can also make time an ally through tokenization, cooperative ownership (buy in now, benefits returned over time), and so on.

3. **Hosting:** hosting data, hosting via a home, providing a place for business to operate, where things happen and what experience happens in that place can be adjusted to increase the value of an experience, product, or relationship.

4. **Service:** doing some type of work: physical, knowledge, creative, etc work in return for something. Bartering services with others can build relationships and businesses even in times and places where money seems in short supply.

5. **Information:** personal data or collective data. Information, good information, can create value, increase efficiency and effectiveness, and build relationships. While you can't sell your shopping habits to your landlord or bank yet, there is an emerging market of data lakes, data commoning, and just simple knowledge sharing that moves value and builds wealth.

6. **Attention:** what one does with their eyeballs, can also be influencer engagement. While advertisers buying your eyeballs can feel incongruent because the ad doesn't fit the needs of viewers, it does pay for the page. Still, attention is a resource that can be directed in even better ways. Make that attention feel more congruent by applying it to purpose, passion, and partnerships.

7. **Social Network:** The value in social networks comes from what happens in relationships and between people. It doesn't have to be captured and locked in by platforms. Engage networks by creating barter and referral opportunities, fostering collaborations that enable the ecosystem to thrive.

This begins to form something of a dashboard of options for creating flows of capital. Dashboards are composed of options and knobs, which will be adjusted as the organization grows from its fundraising in the early stages to another setting for its growth phase and yet a third for its mature phase.

How much do we turn one knob or another?

I invite readers to participate in the creation of these new dashboards by adding their own options and dials to create their dashboards in this collaborative space.

Virginie Glaenzer

Global Lives Dashboard[33]

As an open-source library of videos, the non-profit uses fundraising and volunteers to make 24-hours-in-the-life-of films. Through in kind contributions, volunteers hours, and local participants, Global Lives recruit volunteers who will give their hours and skills, growing their own experience and credibility.

Their non-profit business model streams a movie rather than selling it on DVD as well as selling a book[34]. And places such as art museums host and sponsor the work.

---

[33] https://globallives.org/

[34] https://www.amazon.com/Unheard-Stories-Building-Empathy-Through/dp/0692629734/

Virginie Glaenzer

Currencies (KPIs): Resources (Staff / Money flow). Impact measure.

Knobs of Currents Flow (CHOICES): Freemium / Fundraising / Attention

The Economics of Abundance  Global Lives Project

Abundance Dashboard
OVERALL PERFORMANCE

Currencies
KPIs

Knobs of Currents Flow

 80% Time 74% Service

Reap Community[35] Dashboard

As an online community and SaaS platform, Reap invites entrepreneurs to optimize their business for the new economy by better managing their relationships.

Currencies (KPIs): Resources (time, social network, skills).

Blocks of Currents Flow (CHOICES): Crypto token.

---

[35] https://www.reapcommunity.co/

Virginie Glaenzer

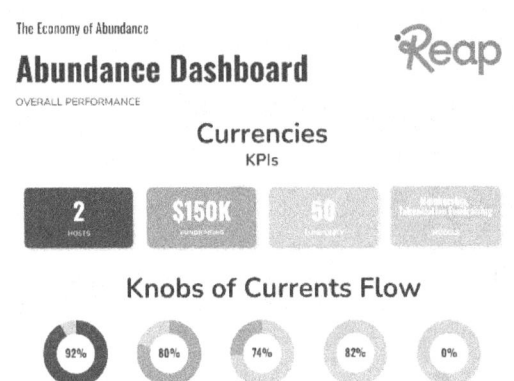

We want to use capital in a way that allows us to move away from tracking and surveillance that make us feel like we live in a petri dish, along with the walled gardens that form the edges of that dish.

We want to keep subsidized participation because it makes sense as a way to enable more people to participate—an equity innovation we appreciate. And, we want that subsidized access to feel congruent with our values and interests.

We also want to move towards economic solutions that make sense in our specific context and enable informed consent for interaction while increasing equitable access.

<u>These equity innovation solutions confront a number of paradoxes and tensions.</u>

Resolving these paradoxes and tensions requires us to address the following questions:

1. Who can pay and who benefits? Who needs it? How do we balance those?
2. Where is the right place for governance to influence the quality and serve a collective interest?
3. What do healthy boundaries look like and where should they be? With whose permission? Acts of generosity expand option space and walls can contain it.
4. How does the system enable feedback without getting bogged down by the response to feedback and administration thereof?
5. We have collapsed the difference between rival and nonrival goods in our marketplaces, twisting non-rival goods into scarcity-based forms to drive compensation for them. Is that necessary, and are there ways around it?

Behavioral economics[36] shows us that our behavior is already being "shaped", and knowing that can help us to navigate consciously in ways that are good for the individual and for the collective.

By examining who participates in a business, understanding the incentives involved, where ownership matters and access can be sufficient, we can understand how cash flow can be hacked for making games last longer and find out how monetization enables a decent life span for the business.

Monetization, or better yet, Wealth-ization, can enable a decent life span for the business.

---

[36] https://en.wikipedia.org/wiki/Nudge_(book)

Virginie Glaenzer

New Forms of Abundant Business Models

The economy of abundance shifts "users" into actively engaging flows by understanding who creates what value and how value gets shared and distributed. Today, consumers generate value but are not capturing their share of returns because our current business models focus more on creating scarcity than distributing value.

The following five business models provide excellent examples of how businesses in the real world can apply the principles of abundance.

1. Pay-As-You-Go

Monthly subscriptions have become a widely used model. When combined with Freemium, Pay-as-you-go models offer more granularity by allowing some participants to pay more and get more. Recently, Patreon enables content and artist creators to run a subscription service and earn a monthly income by providing rewards and perks directly to their subscribers.

2. Freemium

In the freemium model, users who value it most pay for the product while the others benefit from the free version. In other words, a portion of the market pays a premium while others benefit from the freemium. Many applications such as Trello as well as many games use this abundance model. While it is rather common in software, this can also apply to membership models in the brick and mortar world. Premiums can be perks of access, time, or features.

3. Pay-Per-Use

This model lubricates a flow between participants and charges a small fee on the transaction for it. It would be well suited for a field or ecosystem. Real-life examples are Holo and car-sharing. For car-sharing, Zipcar innovated on this model years ago. Their founder, Robin Chase, lays out the method for melding community with organizational infrastructure in Peers, Inc.[37]

4. Pay-For-Parts

Another option would be to pay for the features you want to be added or modified. That could include feature requests or bug fixes. This model can easily be tokenized and lends itself well to technology tools but can also be applied more broadly. Engaging communities in building out capacity seems like an innovation many industries might be primed for.

5. Gratitude Gestures

A gesture of appreciation can have a big impact on your business's bottom line. Gratitude is often followed by reciprocity which is the human need and tendency to want to give back when something is received. Examples of business models include a voluntary financial thank you or a tip jar that can help keep customers coming back.

---

[37] http://www.peersincorporated.com/

CHAPTER SEVEN: EXAMPLES OF ABUNDANT BUSINESSES

Businesses Thriving in Abundance

As people mature the sharing economy ideas of collaboration, there is a way for cooperatives to form collectives that can continuously steer towards abundance rather than get swallowed by demands for profitability.

One method for ensuring enduring abundance is by sharing power through legal structures that helps to create abundance.

⋈ EQUAL EXCHANGE

For example, **Equal Exchange** is a coffee cooperative. You might recognize the Equal Exchange logo if you are a conscious consumer. They are one of the largest cooperatives in the United States. They are so successful that they bought out similar efforts (which were struggling) in order to keep the promise alive. They sell over $80 Million annually.

Cooperatives leverage legal structures to align on shared wealth rather than individual accumulation.

"The legal architecture of organizations and enterprises is, in many respects, the architecture of our economy. Legal structures dictate how wealth flows through our organizations and how decisions are made. Traditional enterprise models are designed to grow the wealth of people who already have wealth, giving all decision-making power to those same individuals. By contrast, cooperatives put wealth and decisions into the hands of workers and consumers, building community well-being and transforming local economies." Sustainable Economies Law Center[38]

---

[38] https://www.theselc.org/cooperatives

Virginie Glaenzer

Community Supported Agriculture (CSAs)[39] and crowdfunding offer paths to abundance by creating alternative pathways to funding that share risk with their fans and consumers. In a CSA, buyers pay upfront, investing in a share at the beginning of the season. Doing so allows them to share risks with farmers and also get the reward of locally grown food because the volume of food delivered can vary based on conditions each year. Farmers benefit by being in a direct relationship with consumers (cutting out middlemen who take a cut) as well as avoiding debt. Many farmers take on debt at the beginning of the season to pay off when the harvest comes in.

---

[39] https://centerforneweconomics.org/newsletters/the-radical-roots-of-csas/

Crowdfunding can make a similar move by funding a project, when the risk is high, and waiting for delivery, helping entrepreneurs navigate early-stage funding.

Technologies assist us with the experience of abundance by creating efficiencies in logistics as well as using machines to help humans.

For example, **Just Drive** is a new project helping deliver medical supplies and medicines to rural areas in Africa. It uses QR codes to coordinate the logistics of local drivers and bicyclists to pick up supplies from medical staging grounds and deliver them to clinics even where there is low internet connectivity. But this is inspired by something that predates our internet age, the dabbawala system of lunch delivery in India, which started in the 1890s has inspired many to rethink how logistics can be a more distributed process, less centralized and more robust.

Distributed ledger technologies are often providing support for all the above options by helping create cross-jurisdictional collectives that can manage a bank account together (DAOs) and use smart contracts to execute work automatically. If you were inspired by the book, *Starfish and the Spider*[40], these distributed ledger approaches might interest you.

People are also working on ramps off of the old economy and onto the new. For example, there are exciting prospects for *exiting community*[41]. Innovation continues in the distributed ledger technology space to create currencies that have a utility within a community and act as an ownership stake while creating financial possibilities for their creators and those that invest in them.

---

[40] https://en.wikipedia.org/wiki/The_Starfish_and_the_Spider

[41] https://www.colorado.edu/lab/medlab/exit-to-community

Outside the crypto world, some companies that are struggling in the changing landscapes of our times offer employee buyouts so that they can shift into employee ownership, which may or may not become a cooperative.

Publix Super Markets is an ESOP[42] which is similar to a cooperative but they are not using the same legal structure. It is where employees buy or earn shares in the company to align their interests and that of other share holders. There are also cases of this being used to hand over ownership to employees which can be especially powerful for companies in distress who would have to layoff a large portion of the workforce if they can't get those employees to agree to terms that would make the business recover.

---

[42] https://www.investopedia.com/terms/e/esop.asp

CONCLUSION

When passing by farms, I am reminded of how agriculture has shaped our society. As technology made farming more productive, more people were freed up to perform other tasks. We grew factories, which meant we became more efficient with machines and required fewer workers. When workers who were managing machines became knowledge workers, the hands-on experience of those workers began to be supplemented by more intellectual power.

These areas were about the hand and the head, as described by Prof. Julian Birkinshaw from the London Business School as the industrial revolution. Two things happened: efficiency reduced meaning in people's lives, spending their days managing machines and doing accounting; while mass production and factory workers craved uniqueness and creativity. This is why we are witnessing a shift towards more heart and a craving for deeper relationships.

The path to abundance requires a shift toward a more heart-centered focus and more meaningful relationships.

We live in an abundant world where the quest for efficiency collides with the need for meaning.

As we look for ways to be more efficient, we also look for meaning in our work, a sense of purpose, a connection with others, and a way to contribute. Efficiency can lead to abundance when we don't compromise on the well-being of people and the need for space for resources to replenish.

To those whose worldview is open to seeing anew, abundance is found everywhere when we challenge our belief in scarcity and remember that most of life happens in cooperation.

I invite you to try new ways of living and focus on what might be possible for you and your family.

You can find inspiration in the world around you.

1. Start looking inward by asking yourself: what is enough for me and the people I care about?
2. Discover your local communities: farmers, producers, artists, etc... Abundance comes from feeling deeply connected and supported by others around us.
3. Join our circle[43] to continue the exploration: Every month, we'll discuss living in abundance and changing our daily habits to adapt to what is possible.
4. Practice seeing abundance by filling out the Abundant Dashboard for your business and your personal life.
5. Join a Co-op or CSA in your area. Buy from co-ops like Ace Hardware.
6. Consider crowdfunding.
7. Play with AI, robotics, and distributed ledger technology.

---

[43] https://www.theabundanceeconomy.com/

A STORY OF ABUNDANCE - CONTINUED.

The day dawned clear and crisp as the sun poured through the window, illuminating the brilliant light filtering through the leaves of the willow tree.

River woke up feeling a little groggy and disoriented.

"I feel tired this morning. We stayed up so late talking. I need to be fully ready to hit the ground running this morning" River said with a smile, "We have the community meeting at eleven-thirty."

"Don't worry. I'll make you a strong coffee. Espresso coming right up!"

At eleven o'clock, the community center door opened. The center was one of those malls, like many across the country, that had been repurposed from a former shopping mall. In the last ten years, most shopping malls had been abandoned as consumers stopped buying for entertainment and ego.

River was sitting outside waiting for the doors to open, reading an article about the how the Florida Keys were recovering. First the article reviewed how the damage became unacceptable.

A decade ago, people finally realized that product waste had reached its peak and things would never be the same. When a tsunami hit part of Florida, the once beautiful beaches of Miami down to the white sand of the keys were ruined. The string of tropical islands stretching about 120 miles off the southern tip of Florida were dramatically affected. Killing more than 1,000 people and causing billions of dollars in damage, but more importantly, it also left behind miles of trash. The beaches and streets were completely covered up with waste. Plastic bottles, paper, cardboard, metals, food wastes, broken computers and printers, a sea of trash, and a massive pile of garbage transformed Miami and its surrounding into a landfill.

The white sand of the Keys was ruined and so was the renowned Miami Beach. Once known as a destination for fishing, boating, snorkeling, and scuba diving, the whole area has transformed into a dumping ground. The shoreline and streets were littered with the remains of fast-pleasure and boredom experiences. These ruins devastated the shoreline, dispelling the notion that there was anything left we could salvage from the old world.

Overnight, people stopped buying products wrapped in wasteful packaging, an economic downturn resulted. Many large corporations were unable to adapt their business model fast enough to survive. Some malls were lucky enough to be transformed into community spaces for meetings, open gyms, farmers' markets, and Trade Me, a new form of borrowing and bartering.

Then the article turned to focus on how things have since changed.

Bartering which had been used for centuries and long before money was invented had made a comeback using global sophisticated techniques. These days, trading was done through Online Auctions and Swap Markets seeded by tools like Ebay, Freecycle, and Craigslist. As people struggled to connect in a world of increasing distance and economic uncertainty, the act of bartering had experienced an unprecedented rise.

River left the page open when Martin interrupted them.

"River, Finely!" Martin called out to his usual customers.

"Good morning Martin", replied River. "How are you feeling today?"

"Very well! Thanks for asking. How about you two?"

They engaged in small talk as they entered the mall and followed the signs *"Community Gathering. Topic: Solutions for Seeds."*

The all-hands community meeting was organized by the non-profit organizations *Surviving Through Seed* and *Need for Seed*, both working to improve seed diversity through seed banks, exchange networks, and educational projects.

Today, each local community throughout the world was expected to take part in the global seed renewal effort because after 150 years of industrial agriculture the soil had degraded to the point that food nutrition was noticeably declining, and it was through individual and small plot gardening that humanity had been able to survive. History had repeated, it seems, when during the second world war people raised chickens and made victory gardens in their backyard to compensate for food scarcity. In 1944, when Belgium and France ran out of food, and famine was threatening both countries, one of the many programs from the United States War Relief Service supported the plan to "rechickenize" France. A few vintage war posters can still be spotted in community malls and today, many people raised chickens out of necessity to feed their family.

"Good morning everyone. Please take your seat. We're going to start in just a few minutes."

River and Finely sat down on a bench, when a young man asked, "May I sit here?"

"Of course," replied River.

"Hi. I'm new here. Could you please tell me how this works?", asked the man.

"Hi, welcome to our community! I'm River.

"Nice to meet you, River. I'm Brandon."

"Nice to meet you Brandon. So today, the all-hand meeting is about our seed capacity. We'll share facts, context, and emotions and then we'll engage in question rounds. After that, we'll be paired with other people - in small groups to develop a proposal for our values and purpose. Once submitted to the community, we'll vote and each take on responsibilities and tasks like participatory budgeting."

"That's amazing. I've never heard of a town

being managed this way."

"Well, many of us no longer want to be told what to do and be part of those hierarchical or political organizations. We want our voice to be heard in our community."

"I see," said Brandon, "I've heard about workers and multi-stakeholder cooperatives using decentralized leadership structures. It seems they create a lot more transparency and trustworthy systems."

River added, "Yes, they do. We are all more interdependent and interconnected than we think we are."

Brandon felt intrigued. "What do you..?" Brandon couldn't finish his question as the community presenter asked for everyone's attention.

"Thank you everyone for coming today. We are going to start by presenting who participates in the seed programs, what their incentives are, where ownership matters, and where access can be sufficient. The problem we are going to try to resolve today is that we are facing a dilemma which we'll present in a brief moment."

After an hour of presentation, the round of questions from the participants started.

"How do we replace our current system without removing the positives that previous generations achieved through ordered society?" asked a young woman.

"How can cash flow be hacked for making our game last longer?" added an older individual.

After responding to many questions, the presenter invited participants to form small groups in order to digest the discussion and reflect on their own understanding and values.

Brandon, River, Finely and Martin were assigned to the same group. Following a short introduction to each other, the group engaged in a lively conversation.

Finely started, "If I understand correctly, we're concerned about the long-term effects of a lack of seed diversity on our soil. Is that right?"

"Yes and it's not just that." added Martin, "We want to provide one type of seed that works well in our local climate, but by producing more of that one seed we may be homogenizing the animal species that thrive in this region. And that could create problems for our community in the long run."

"We have the technology to enhance the agricultural potential of plants by overcoming their natural weaknesses," Brandon responded "Why not use it?"

Finely interjected, "It's not that simple. We need to create an inclusive ecosystem in which the soil is effectively cultivated so that all seeds have the potential to thrive for our community and next generations to prepare for a more diverse, inclusive, and profitable future."

A quiet space opened up, and the group's attention turned to the energy of the room. The community topic was causing unease and participants were forced to reconsider their own needs versus those of the community at large.

After a few minutes of silence, Brandon asked, "How do we balance what we need today versus what our community needs in the future?"

"I really appreciate your question," River added, "I feel it's inevitable to discuss how we can consume and organize differently in order to make use of this abundance so that everyone has enough. Once we gain clarity on that, solutions will become evident."

River added, in a soft voice, "A seed is not a complete or finished product. It is both finished and unfinished."

ABOUT THE AUTHOR

Virginie Glaenzer

As a conscious leader and successful serial entrepreneur, Virginie designs digital marketing and sales funnel strategies that drive sustainability and help, leaders and teams navigate complexity with confidence and clarity of thought.

She dedicates her work to improving people's lives by maximizing their efforts and making their intentions a reality. Promoting emerging leadership trends and evolving leaders' relationships with others is what Virginie excels at. She is the co-author of the book "The Leadership Singularity" and the host of the podcast "AcornOak Pass the Mic", a podcast that aims to bring compassion and conscious leadership to business and in our personal lives. Originally from France, she moved to the US in 1999, co-founded three tech starts-up, and began her journey to immerse herself in conscious leadership training in various disciplines such as psychology, wisdom traditions, awareness, and mindfulness practices. Today, Virginie is currently exploring Web3 as a user, builder, and fractional CMO for her clients. You can find Virginie on Twitter at @virginieg, where she engages with the communities at www.acornoak.net and www.ReapCommunity.co.

I'm grateful for the support and contribution of: Jean M. Russell, a social ecosystem designer, culture hacker, and the founder of the thrivability movement and co-founder of Thrivable Society. Jean's work on thrivability, innovation, philanthropy, and cultural shifts has been highlighted in the Economist, Harvard Business Review, Stanford Social Innovation Review, and Worldchanging. She received an honorable mention on the enrichlist, as one of the top 200 people of all time "whose contributions enrich paths to sustainable futures."
https://www.jeanmrussell.com/

PERSONAL NOTES

www.ingramcontent.com/pod-product-compliance
Lightning Source LLC
Chambersburg PA
CBHW071405210526
45465CB00001B/265